Printed in the United States of America

First Printing, 2017

Educational Partners International, LLC

105 Whitson Avenue, Swannanoa, NC 28778

LAUNCH YOUR CLASSROOM MANAGEMENT!

CREATING A WELL-RUN CLASSROOM

ANTHONY SCANNELLA
SHARON MCCARTHY

CONTRIBUTORS

Executive Editor - Andrés V. Martín

Developmental Editor - Johnny M. Penley

Copyeditor - Shannon Roberts

Lead Instructional Designer - Ryan Hennessee

Instructional Designer - Kristina Lunsford

Cover Designer - Anna Berger

Book Design and Layout - Andrés V. Martín & Anna Berger

Production Manager - Kimberly Daggerhart

Production Editor - Jessica Boyd

Video Production - Johnny M. Penley

To all the teachers that invited us into their classrooms.

It's the teacher that makes the difference, not the classroom.

MICHAEL MORPURGO

CONTENT

PREFACE

About the Book

Launch Your Classroom Management! : Creating a Well-Run Classroom is a book for teachers who want to set up their classrooms for success using fast, powerful techniques that maximize student learning. Inside, you'll find some of the most effective ways to begin the school year and build an environment that encourages student growth. We've transformed years of classroom practice and instructional theory into practical advice you can implement now. From learning about your school to building positive relationships with the people you interact with, *Launch Your Classroom!* will help prepare you for some of the most significant challenges in your teaching career.

About the Series

The *Launch Your Classroom!* Series provides actionable professional development strategies for educators. This is why every professional development book we offer provides a highly visual guide that delivers fast, powerful, and actionable strategies in a way that is easy to understand. Everything we cover is meant to be something that you can use right away. In that spirit, we present you with only the most important information so you can make the biggest impact possible with the limited time and resources you have.

Every *Launch Your Classroom!* book is focused on finding ways to simplify complicated concepts. We use visuals to help make ideas more concrete and videos to further illustrate key concepts. We provide options for different learning styles!

How to Read This Book

We recommend you start by reading the entire book from front to back. Then, as you continue teaching, you can revisit sections as you need them. We also suggest that you keep *Launch Your Classroom!* nearby while you're in the classroom so you can reference parts that relate to the skills you're currently developing. As you progress through each chapter, you'll notice we communicate a lot of information using infographics and Rocket Boosters.

WHAT ARE ROCKET BOOSTERS?

As you progress through each chapter, you'll notice we communicate a lot of information using infographics and Rocket Boosters. Rocket Boosters are blocks of valuable information throughout the book that provide you with further resources about a topic. We divide Rocket Boosters into five categories:

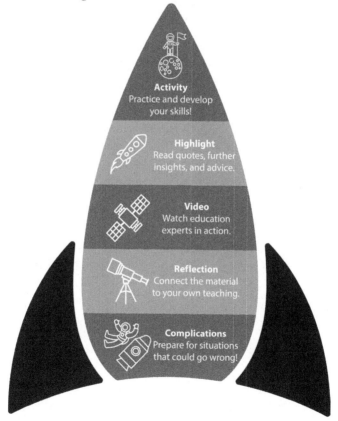

Activity
Practice and develop your skills!

Highlight
Read quotes, further insights, and advice.

Video
Watch education experts in action.

Reflection
Connect the material to your own teaching.

Complications
Prepare for situations that could go wrong!

Important Note: Rocket Boosters have links to our YouTube channel where you can find *Launch Your Classroom!* video resources. All video resources are also available here:

https://www.YouTube.com/EducationalPartnersInternational

PREPARE FOR LAUNCH

INTRODUCTION

Start Here

Whether you're a veteran or rookie, you're sure to have feelings of both fear and excitement about the first day of school. For many teachers, feeling unprepared can be overwhelming. The first day of school is fast approaching, and if you're not ready, your students will know it.

Teachers who have been in the profession for a couple of years can tell you it's never as bad as you imagine. Typically, the pressure you're putting on yourself is a sign of how much you care about doing a great job. Of course, you already know the value of being as prepared as possible—you did pick up this book, after all!

Often, new teachers face a steep learning curve that can directly impact student achievement. We've spent years working with teachers new to the American K-12 classroom. We've worked with teachers of all subjects across all grade levels. As we developed this book, we observed their transition into their classrooms and identified areas where they could benefit from professional development. As you progress through this book, each chapter will focus on critical strategies to help you deal with the challenges you're most likely to face.

We'd like to introduce you to Dr. Anthony Scannella and Sharon McCarthy, educational consultants and authors who've devoted their lives to improving educational systems across the United States of America. They believe in a student-first philosophy and understand how critical the teacher is to providing opportunities for learning. They've helped thousands of teachers develop in their professional capacity.

We look forward to working with you as you launch your classroom management this school year, and we hope that you find this book to be an extremely effective resource!

INTRODUCING TONY AND SHARON

Our professional development materials are more than just books. In *Launch Your Classroom!*, you will have access to exclusive video content of your authors and educational experts, Dr. Anthony Scannella and Sharon McCarthy. These videos enhance the material in this book, providing valuable resources, demonstrations, and opportunities for further learning.

To watch this video, please visit:
https://youtu.be/I1H3IWGcD8Y

PART ONE
RULES AND CONSEQUENCES

STRUCTURES FOR A WELL RUN CLASSROOM

Maintaining order in the classroom and ensuring students remain on task can be a real challenge for a new teacher. Classrooms can be unpredictable places! You can make your classroom more predictable by setting rules and showing students the benefits of following them. Your rules will tell students how you expect them to behave.

Maintaining a disciplined and productive classroom requires mastering three elements:

- **Employing Classroom Management**
- **Designing Effective Rules**
- **Choosing Appropriate Consequences**

In this part, you'll learn how experienced classroom managers create effective instructional spaces, how to work with your students to craft rules that reinforce important values, and when to use different consequences for different rule violations.

ONE
EMPLOYING CLASSROOM MANAGEMENT

We'll begin by taking a look at how effective classroom managers operate in the classroom. In the next infographic, we break down the most powerful habits you can develop to improve the way your students function in the classroom.

THE SEVEN HABITS OF EFFECTIVE CLASSROOM MANAGERS

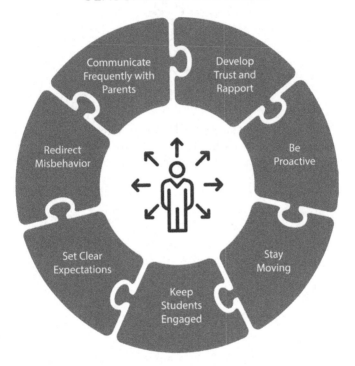

- **Develop Trust and Rapport:** Trust and rapport are the foundation for positive relationships. When students respect and trust you, you'll see a much greater commitment to productivity and good behavior. Learn their names, discover their interests and backgrounds, and find out their goals and future plans.
- **Be Proactive:** When you find yourself constantly responding to classroom issues, you likely aren't being an effective instructor. Stay ahead of the problems by emphasizing planning and prevention. Anticipate issues before they become distractions. Have a back-up plan.

- **Stay Moving:** Good classroom managers move about the room on a regular basis—they don't sit behind the desk or isolate themselves at the front of the class for the entire period.
- **Keep Students Engaged:** Bored or distracted students turn into misbehaving students very quickly. Keep your class's attention by varying your teaching methods: start each class differently, keep lectures brief, employ short tasks and activities, and keep transitions simple.
- **Set Clear Expectations:** Often after a poor performance or misbehavior, students will profess a lack of understanding of the expectations for the assignment or behavior norms. Anticipate this response by spending time early in the semester clearly laying out your expectations. Don't be afraid to review these expectations frequently.
- **Redirect Misbehavior:** Calling students out for misbehavior isn't enough; you need to get them back on task. Instead of telling them what not to do, tell them what they should be doing.
- **Communicate Frequently with Parents:** Skillful teachers know the importance of establishing and maintaining relationships with students' parents. Contact parents early in the school year. Take advantage of open houses and back-to-school nights. Remember, parents must be informed when their child misbehaves, but they relish and appreciate good news, whether it's behavioral or academic in nature.

CLASSROOM MANAGEMENT DEFINED

"Classroom Management" is a phrase beginning teachers often hear tossed around. In a nutshell, the term refers to the techniques used by teachers to keep students disciplined and productive. As you can imagine, classroom management is critical to how your class functions.

What's important to grasp; however, is that classroom management isn't just about responding to misbehavior. Indeed, the effective teacher will spend just as much time creating frameworks and procedures that prevent problems from happening in the first place.

HABITS IN ACTION

As a teacher, some of your most valuable resources are the colleagues who teach near you. A great way to help strengthen the effectiveness of your classroom management is by watching your colleagues manage their classes!

For this activity, choose a teacher in your school to observe. Pre-arrange with your supervisor and chosen colleague a time when you'll be able to watch them teach a lesson. Make sure you allow time to study the transitions into and out of the lesson. Using the "Seven Habits of Effective Classroom Managers" framework, observe the teacher and their students, and note specific examples of each of the seven habits in action.

1. What techniques make this teacher an effective classroom manager?
2. What did you observe that you can put into practice immediately?

HOLD STUDENTS ACCOUNTABLE

It's important to remember that classroom management isn't about punishing students: it's about providing a foundation of conduct and behavior that creates an environment where they can learn and excel. In this video, Tony shares a compelling story about holding students accountable and working together to develop their learning.

To watch this video, please visit:
https://youtu.be/tRwUIM8dSVs

THE WEAKEST LINK

Review the "Seven Habits of Effective Classroom Managers." Now, choose one habit you feel is your "weakest link." If you're having difficulty determining which of the habits is your weakest link, consider your daily routine. You should be able to think of specific actions that are part of your typical teaching style and which actions demonstrate each habit. If you find you're having difficulty thinking of exactly how you demonstrate a particular habit, that's your weakest link!

Once you've identified it, you're ready to begin. Memorize the habit's name and make sure you understand the habit's explanation. Then, approach your day as normal. Here's the trick: in every routine action you perform, from taking attendance to direct instruction, perform it with a constant, mindful focus on your weakest link. Pay special attention to how the habit, or absence of it, affects your day.

Next, answer these questions:

1. What parts of your day were most impacted by your weakest link?
2. If you had complete mastery of all seven habits, how would that part of your day look? What would be different?
3. Are there any steps that you can take today toward developing your weakest link into one of your most powerful habits?
4. You'll find that as you improve one of these habits, your weakest link may change. By periodically revisiting this activity, you will continue to develop your overall ability to manage a classroom.

TWO
DESIGNING EFFECTIVE RULES

Now that you know the basics of classroom management, it's time to consider how to design a set of rules to govern your classroom. In this section, we'll take a look at what makes rules effective, how to root your rules in values, and the importance of working with your students to create rules together.

FIVE GUIDELINES FOR DESIGNING EFFECTIVE RULES

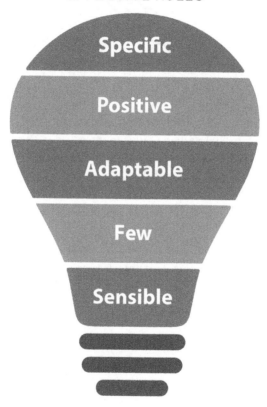

- **Specific:** Rules need to be as specific as possible.
- **Positive:** State your rules in the positive rather than the negative. For example, instead of "don't yell in class," say, "speak quietly in class."
- **Adaptable:** Periodically evaluate your rules and their effectiveness. If at any time a rule doesn't seem to be working, change the rule!
- **Few:** Keep your rules few in number. You should have no more than five rules.
- **Sensible:** Make rules that make sense!

EXAMPLES OF CLASSROOM RULES:

- Treat others with respect at all times.
- Listen to the teacher when s/he speaks.
- Ask for help when you need it.
- Be prepared every day with required items.
- Respect other people's property.
- Listen and follow directions.
- Raise your hand before speaking or leaving your seat.
- Respect your classmates and your teacher.
- Keep hands, feet, and objects to yourself.

WORK WITH STUDENTS TO CREATE CLASSROOM RULES

We highly recommend you work with your students to design your rules. Discussing and planning this with students at the beginning of the year gives them an investment and sense of ownership in the code of conduct to which they will be held accountable.

A great way to frame this exercise is around values. Consider, both alone and with your students, what values are important to guarantee a positive and productive classroom. You should try to end up with no more than three or four, ensuring that the rules you develop based on those values will be similarly few in number.

However, don't be afraid to generate a lot of potential rules and values with your students and together, combine and refine them down to a manageable number. Entertain discussion among students who might have different opinions about the possible values. The more possibilities you record, the more you ensure that every student's voice is heard, that they have participated in the process, and that they have a sense of investment in the rulemaking.

Each value and rule should be explained, discussed, and demonstrated so all students have a complete understanding of how to behave in class. For example, if safety is a chosen classroom value, you could start a discussion on what makes a classroom safe. During the discussion, the students will evaluate different options, and then you can lead them to a final version of the classroom rules. This process empowers your students by directly involving them in rulemaking and gets them talking among themselves about behavioral expectations.

When deciding on values, encourage your students to identify values they admire in the people in their lives. Family, friends, and community members can be wonderful role models for students and exemplars of positive values. Similarly, don't hesitate to point out examples of values modeled by the people in your school—not just teachers, but administrators, custodians, and staff.

EXAMPLES OF VALUES:

- Safety
- Responsibility
- Respect
- Curiosity
- Kindness
- Integrity
- Collaboration
- Adaptability

DESIGN RULES WITH STUDENTS

If you want your students to not only follow the classroom rules but become invested in them, a very effective strategy is partnering with your students to design the rules together. Tony and Sharon demonstrate how to perform this community-building exercise of choosing classroom values, refining those values into rules, and synthesizing those rules into a list.

To watch this video, please visit:
https://youtu.be/Fs-JDyMwy_M

VALUES FOR LEARNING

Most teachers would say they have "values." The question is which values are important enough to be the basis upon which to make your classroom rules? Which values would you want all your students to exhibit in their lives as adults? Create a list of values that answer this question. Then, rank them in order of importance.

Now consider: do you have enough important values listed to create five rules for your classroom?

GIVE ME FIVE

Building classroom rules with your class can take some time, but it is a vital part of student "buy-in" and will have a massive impact on how you want your class to run. As an educator, you probably already have a set of rules you feel are best for your class. The key to making rules together; however, is writing down the suggestions of your students, then shaping their rules into a set that satisfies your requirements as well as your students' stated needs.

For this activity, imagine you're creating a set of rules with your class. After you ask your students for recommendations, you have the following list:

- Don't Talk
- Be Nice
- Don't Run
- Do Your Work on Time
- Do Your Homework
- Don't Hit Each Other
- Don't Lie
- Keep the Room Clean
- Clean Your Desk
- Don't Talk in Line
- Don't Come Late to Class

Using this list, establish a set of classroom rules.

Do the rules you have created follow the "Five Guidelines for Designing Effective Rules?" If not, what should you change to make it work?

THREE
CHOOSING APPROPRIATE
CONSEQUENCES

Classroom rules provide a guide for how students should conduct themselves at school, and sooner or later some students will violate those rules. In this section, we'll take a look at how to choose consequences that are appropriate in proportion to the broken rule and some techniques for recording student behavior.

What Makes an Appropriate Consequence?

Consequences should relate directly to the rule violated and be as logical as possible. The idea is not to punish the student with unfair or severe consequences but for the student to learn responsibility and reduce instances of misbehavior. Rules and their consequences should make your class run more smoothly.

For example, imagine one of your classroom values is "Respect" and the associated rule is "Respect all classroom property and materials." A student caught defacing a desk shouldn't receive an enforced silent lunch period—the consequence has nothing to do with the rule being violated. Instead, have the student clean the desks after class—then the rule and consequence are aligned.

EXAMPLES OF CONSEQUENCES:

- A verbal reminder of the rule and value when it is first broken
- A written reminder when the rule is violated again
- A one-on-one conference with the teacher
- A behavior contract
- A phone call home to parents after multiple infractions
- A conference with the school administrator in severe circumstances
- Providing a student with recovery space to bring themselves under control

LOGICAL CONSEQUENCES

Do your consequences make sense? A lack of logic in the repercussions for rule-breaking can lead to increased misbehavior. In this video, Tony brings you into his simulated classroom environment to demonstrate how to make sure your consequences are aligned with the nature of the misbehavior.

To watch this video, please visit:
https://youtu.be/beYhdNiAPP4

HOW TO MAINTAIN
TRUST AND RAPPORT

The quickest way to destroy the trust and rapport you've built with a student is to humiliate them in front of peers. You should expect any student to react badly to open criticism in front of other students.

To protect your students and manage a classroom at the same time, you must:

- Carry out disciplinary actions quietly and quickly
- Keep your voice calm during student misbehavior
- Avoid saying anything sarcastic or condescending

If a student responds negatively to a disciplinary action carried out with the right amount of discretion, you can regain control of the situation by explaining how you must be fair to all students. You might say, "How would you feel if I disciplined you but didn't discipline another classmate who did the same thing? I'd be showing favoritism if I give you special treatment." Most students in this situation will agree that this is the fair thing to do. Some students will agree to avoid the appearance of a teacher giving them individual special treatment.

In addition, you should try to recognize good behavior when you see it. Imagine that every student has a "recognition piggy bank." When you recognize students' great habits, you make a deposit into their piggy banks. When you discipline students, you're making a withdrawal. Like any bank account, a recognition piggy bank should have a positive balance! Recognize your students' achievements every chance you get to build goodwill over time.

"APPROPRIATE" CONSEQUENCES

Sometimes, we use a word so often it loses the full power of its meaning. What does the word "appropriate" mean to you? Now look it up in the dictionary. What does the word "appropriate" actually mean?

Most definitions will show that when something is appropriate, it is suitable or proper in the circumstance. With this in mind, is an "appropriate consequence" based on the behavior that it follows, or is it based on the student who has exhibited the behavior? Could it be based on both?

Imagine two students were caught stealing food from the cafeteria. What appropriate consequence would you choose? What if one of the students lives in a home where food is scarce and regular meals are not dependable? Does that change your appropriate consequence? Did you make any assumptions that would lead you to an inappropriate consequence?

CONNECT CONSEQUENCES

We always want consequences to align with the rules being violated. We want students to see their actions and behavior as choices, learning responsibility through logical and appropriate reinforcement. In this activity, we'll test your ability to use appropriate consequences. Try connecting the example of misbehavior to a consequence you feel naturally aligns with it:

1. Talking in the hallway on the way to lunch
2. Defacing a desk
3. Texting repeatedly on a cell phone
4. Kicking someone during a recess soccer game
5. Putting toilet paper all over the mirrors in the bathroom
6. Forgetting a homework assignment

a. Calling the student's parent from their cell phone
b. Requiring the student to work on homework during breaks
c. Walking from the classroom to the lunchroom beside the teacher
d. Cleaning the bathroom with the custodian
e. Cleaning the classroom desks after class
f. The student must sit by themselves during recess

Key: 1:c, 2:e, 3:a, 4:f, 5:d, 6:b

TRACK AND RECORD
STUDENT BEHAVIOR

An important part of managing student behavior is keeping a record of it. This kind of data can be beneficial when discussing the student's behavior with school administrators and parents. And if a situation ever escalates to legal action, a written record of student misbehavior and consequences is an invaluable tool to have on your side.

A great way to record this is through a behavior checklist. To create the checklist, make a table for each student, either digitally or on sheets of paper. The columns contain the date of the infraction, the rule violated, and any relevant descriptive comments. Use these comments to record what transpired and how you responded. Here is a sample table:

Student Name	Date	Rule Violated	Comments
Quintin S.	4/11	Respect fellow classmates.	Quintin was given a verbal warning after pulling a classmate's hair and asked to apologize.
Quintin S.	4/13	Listen to the teacher when he/she is speaking.	Quintin continued to talk during instructions after a verbal warning, and was given silent lunch.

KEEP BEHAVIORAL RECORDS CONFIDENTIAL!

It is important to keep behavioral records confidential to protect your student's privacy. In our example, each student has their own table. That way, in the event you need to share the behavioral record with an administrator or parent, you will only be sharing the information relevant to the student in question. When sharing your behavioral checklist with your principal or assistant principals, be sure to include a copy of your classroom rules and consequences.

OPTIMIZE YOUR
BEHAVIORAL RECORDS

Written behavioral records are a crucial part of teacher documentation in the classroom. Review your current strategies for recording student behavior and consider the following: If you were to need documentation on a student quickly, would your collected data be specific, useful, and easily understood? Could it be used comprehensively—meaning, would it be helpful in understanding the child academically and behaviorally? Would it be useful for testing purposes, during parent or principal conferences, and with school specialists? How could you adjust your tracking techniques for optimal use?

CONCLUSION

As you prepare to launch your classroom, remember that making effective rules and consequences isn't about punishing students. It's about creating a system that supports learning, celebrates enthusiasm and engagement, and controls and limits misbehavior.

Also, remember that a classroom changes over the course of a school year and can take on a life of its own, so it's important to review classroom rules and consequences periodically. Are they still working? If not, don't be afraid to change them to better reflect the classroom community.

Now that you've created the framework for effective classroom management, we need to discuss the tools you'll use to keep your classroom operating on schedule: procedures and transitions.

PART TWO
PROCEDURES AND TRANSITIONS

TAKING CONTROL WITH PREDICTABLE RULES

Rules and consequences govern classroom behavior, but procedures and transitions determine how a class operates from day to day. Procedures show students how to perform classroom activities while transitions show them how to shift between activities. Great procedures and transitions allow students to predict and plan their school day. In time, these plans become routines that improve both student learning and teaching effectiveness.

In this part, we will discuss:

- **Increasing Your Instructional Time**
- **Creating Procedures for a Well-Run Classroom**
- **Teaching and Rehearsing Classroom and School Transitions**
- **Keeping Your Students Learning**

Successful teachers plan for, insist on, and actively teach strong procedures and transitions within their classrooms. As you develop your procedures and transitions, consider this useful guiding question: "How can I set up and manage my classroom so my students know what to do and how and when to do it?"

In many classrooms, behavior problems tend to pop up during the chaos of transitioning between activities.

Instead of giving in to chaos, you can take control and stop these problems before they ever begin. We'll show you transition techniques to get your students focused and excited about what they're learning next, which can win back more instruction time and ensure that your classroom runs smoothly.

RULES OR PROCEDURES?

The main difference between rules and procedures is that rules have attached consequences. A student who fails to follow a procedure should not face a consequence but should be reminded and retrained on how to execute the procedure.

INTRODUCTION TO PROCEDURES AND TRANSITIONS

There's a link between student behavior, performance, achievement, and the procedures and transitions that govern a classroom. In this video, Sharon makes a case for designing your classroom procedures early on and taking the time to think about how you want your classroom to run.

To watch this video, please visit:
https://youtu.be/R7l94lv8dNs

FOUR

INCREASING YOUR INSTRUCTIONAL TIME

The most valuable and compelling reason to set up procedures and transitions in your classroom is the amount of instructional time that can be reclaimed. Imagine if you could get an entire extra week of instructional time during your school year. Impossible? Not with effective procedures and transitions.

For example, let's imagine you have six major transitions between activities in your daily class routine, and let's further imagine it takes your students five minutes to navigate these transitions. Perhaps they take too long to put away the classroom calculators, retrieve books from cupboards, or return from lunch. If you develop a transition that reduces that time from five minutes to two and instruct your students on how to perform that transition, you'll begin to see some exciting results.

FIVE STEPS TO REDUCE TIME SPENT ON TRANSITIONS

To begin earning your extra week of instructional time, follow these simple rules about introducing, teaching, and reteaching classroom transitions:

- **Explain:** Make sure your instructions are clear.
- **Demonstrate:** Show students what you expect to see them do.
- **Rehearse:** Give your students the opportunity to practice.
- **Display:** Make it visible to keep it in your students' minds.
- **Reteach:** When necessary, help your students remember.

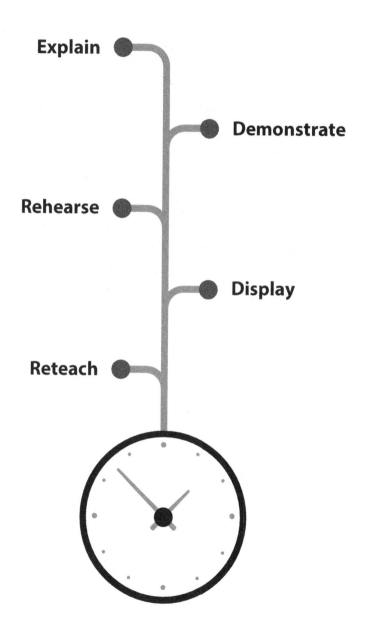

Explain

Demonstrate

Rehearse

Display

Reteach

WASTED TIME ADDS UP!

Three extra minutes per transition, multiplied by six transitions a day, multiplied by, on average, one hundred and eighty school days is over eight school days' worth of instructional time reclaimed by the end of the year.

FIVE

CREATING PROCEDURES FOR A WELL-RUN CLASSROOM

Even if students rarely admit it, having classroom procedures to follow can be a relief. With expectations for activities, events, and transitions in place, students and teachers are free to be more creative and fully engaged in the class because everyone knows exactly what's expected of them. When students know what to do and how to do it, they're more likely to engage in positive social interaction and invest in their learning.

There are many, many aspects of the classroom for which you need to ensure procedures are in place. From the start of class each day to students gathering materials, bathroom visits, seating, using the pencil sharpener, it's easy to feel overwhelmed by the number of procedures needed.

To begin crafting your procedures, you need to take a self-assessment to determine which procedures you already have in place, which ones you need, and the integrity of both.

Use the following Procedural Questions List to inventory your procedures. As you read each item, ask yourself these questions:

- Is there a current procedure in place?
- Are students following this procedure?
- Are the directions posted in a prominent place?
- Does the procedure need to be taught?

Take notes when you see an opportunity to improve the procedure.

Procedural Questions List

Start of Class

- How should students enter the room?
- Do the students put their things away when they enter or when you call their row?
- Is there a transition exercise?

Classroom Management

- When and how can a student leave the room?
- How do students get materials?
- Who is responsible for which job(s)?

Classwork

- How should students format their papers?
- What do students who finish early do?
- How will students who are absent get their make-up work?

Learning Centers

- How many students are allowed at a center at a time?
- How is time managed at each center?
- How many centers are students expected to cycle through?
- How do you keep track of what the student has completed and still needs to do?
- How do students keep track of what they have completed and still need to do?
- Are step sheets displayed for the centers?

Homework

- How do your students turn in homework?
- How is it graded?
- Where will the assignments be posted?

End of Class

- Does the bell end the class or do you?
- Do your students line up or leave individually?
- What kind of notification do you require for a student to be dismissed early?

Other

- What is the procedure for a fire drill?
- What are your expectations for students when a substitute teacher is necessary?
- What is your lunchtime procedure?

EMERGENCY DRILLS AND PROCEDURES

Most schools have required emergency drills that you'll be called on to conduct from time to time. Depending on your geographic location, schools have unique safety challenges. In the United States, midwestern states are likely to see increased tornado activity. If you're close to the Atlantic coast or the Gulf of Mexico, the probability of a hurricane increases.

Emergencies are not limited to natural disasters. However unlikely it may be, most schools also have a plan for hostile or unwelcome visitors. The potential for harm in any one of these emergencies warrants treating emergency drills and procedures with the utmost respect.

Typically, schools will practice required emergency drills consistently throughout the school year. Most emergency drills include procedures that practice the school's ability to respond to basic threats. Most often, there are three types of responses:

- **Evacuation** - These responses move people away from immediate threats such as a fire or tsunami.
- **Lockdown** - These responses isolate people from threats of violence like trespassers or armed intruders.

- **Seeking Shelter** - These responses isolate the inside of the school from the outside to limit the exposure to environmental threats, such as chemical contaminants or earthquakes.

It's your responsibility to make sure your students can follow the procedures in each type of emergency drill. Also, you may be asked to be part of a rapid responder system or other emergency management plan. If this is the case, take your responsibility very seriously. Either way, you play a critical part in ensuring the safety of your students in an emergency.

Finally, always follow any instruction given to you by emergency responders such as firefighters, paramedics, and police officers. These individuals have completed advanced training to respond to any emergency.

SIX

TEACHING AND REHEARSING CLASSROOM AND SCHOOL TRANSITIONS

The most significant loss of instructional time occurs when we ask our students to transition from one activity to another. It's very easy to lose focus when you stop doing one thing and move to something different, and in school, we must transition many, many times each day.

When moving from one activity to another, students require time to readjust their thinking. How you handle these transitions is crucial to the effective management of your disciplined learning environment. Recall the 80/20 rule: teaching your students the proper transitions and procedures will be a large part of the 20% of the time you use to consciously create your desired classroom culture.

To effectively present transitions to your students, follow these rules:

- **Teach:** Students won't know what to do unless you tell them. Spend as much time as you need early in the school year to teach and establish the expected procedures and transitions. You'll earn back this time and more when your classroom runs like a well-oiled machine.

- **Rehearse:** Likewise, don't expect students to perform perfectly without practice. Once you've introduced the procedures and transitions, allow your students time to rehearse.
- **Post Visually:** Even after learning and rehearsing procedures and transitions, students will sometimes need a reminder or reference point. Post classroom procedures where everyone can see them. Visual directions (as opposed to oral) provide greater clarity and double the length of memory retention. Use graphics as well as words; not only do some of your students think in pictures, graphics add visual interest and engagement. Keep the directions in a consistent place!

THE POWER OF VISUALIZATION

When leading your students through transition and procedure, why not use the technique of seasoned athletes? Athletes employ vivid, highly detailed visualizations and run-throughs of their entire upcoming performance, engaging all their senses in the mental rehearsal.

When we visualize, our brains are training for the actual performance. When you imagine a task, the motor control, attention, perception, planning, and memory centers of the brain all engage.

Begin by introducing a specific task to your class, such as moving from the classroom to the cafeteria. Mention all the behaviors they should engage in during their walk – eyes in front, single file, silent, hands at their sides – whatever your expectations are. Tell the students to imagine the walk to the cafeteria and visualize it as if they're currently doing it.

Encourage the students to use as many senses as they can in their visualizations. Prompt them with questions: who are you standing next to? What are you wearing? Can you smell the cafeteria? What sounds do you hear in the hallway? Then, ask students to share what they're experiencing.

After students have shared their visualizations, pick and choose the clearest visualizations and synthesize them together into a single, standardized experience.

During the first weeks of school, practice visualization each time you're about to perform a procedure or transition and make any corrections or changes necessary. The more students get used to the process, the more you'll be able to apply it to different areas of the classroom.

VISUALIZE YOUR PROCEDURES AND TRANSITIONS

In this video, Sharon demonstrates the power of using visualization as a tool for students to learn and comprehend classroom procedures and transitions. This technique can significantly assist with providing your students clear expectations for how to perform everyday activities.

To watch this video, please visit:
https://youtu.be/EyTX_cX2BMA

SEVEN
KEEPING YOUR STUDENTS LEARNING

Effective management of classroom procedures and transitions earns an educator more instructional time per school year. Now it's time to make sure your students spend that time as productively as possible. One set of tools for ensuring productivity is Anchor Activities.

Anchor Activities are activities students have been trained to work on once they finish classroom assignments. These activities keep students learning and significantly reduce downtime in your classroom.

These activities should not be busywork, however. They should be devised ahead of time and related to your current lesson or unit, reinforcing the material you're currently teaching. The most important aspects of an Anchor Activity are represented on the following infographic:

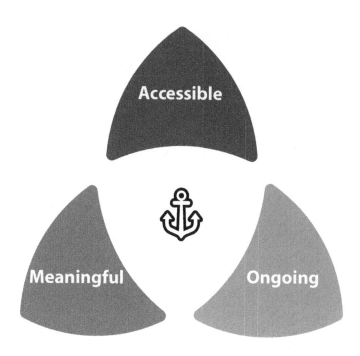

- **Accessible:** Students should be able to jump directly into an Anchor Activity. Every student should have a chance to participate.

- **Meaningful:** Students should never spend valuable class time on busywork. Anchor Activities should be engaging and relate to what's being learned.

- **Ongoing:** Students should be able to use Anchor Activities to fill downtime in the class. You should consider both individual and group Anchor Activities.

Anchor Activity Examples

You should always create Anchor Activities that are related to your lessons and units. Examples of effective Anchor Activities for different subjects include:

Math

- *Problems of the Week:* Students are given a series of problems at the beginning of the week to work on throughout the week as time allows.
- *Road Trip:* Students plan a road trip across the United States. Using a map - paper or digital - students measure distances and add up the total mileage. How many days would they be gone? What would be the cost of gas? Motel rooms? Meals?
- *Money, Money:* Students research the history of currency and trade, and prepare a short report.

Science

- *Science Heroes:* Students research important scientists from history and write short paragraphs about how their work connects to the current unit.
- *Ripped from the Headlines:* Students read current magazines, newspapers, and electronic media related to the current scientific topic of study.
- *Necessity is the Mother of Invention:* Students are given a list of inventions and breakthroughs related to the current science lesson and asked to answer: "What problems did this invention solve? What process of thinking led scientists to create it?"

Social Studies

- *Letters from History:* Students imagine themselves to be a famous figure from history, and write letters about the current events of the lesson. Students can work in pairs, writing letters back and forth.
- *How Would They Handle It?:* Students research current issues of interest and imagine how historical leaders would have responded to or solved them.
- *Laws of the Land:* Students create a fictional country set in the same time period as the lesson. What laws would they choose to govern their nation? What would their relationship be to the rest of the world in this era?

As you can see, the possibilities are endless. Use this list as a spark to ignite your imagination, and devise Anchor Activities that are meaningful and based on your lessons.

REVISE THE ANCHOR

As this chapter emphasizes, Anchor Activities should be accessible, meaningful, and ongoing. Re-think the activities below such that they become an effective Anchor Activity for the subject they're associated with:

- English: Read a self-chosen chapter book.
- Math: Color a picture using mixed color patterns.
- Science: Create a dialogue between two scientists.

For each activity, analyze what key components are missing. What can be added or changed in the directions to make the activity successful?

Can you adapt any of these anchor activities for your class?

WORST-CASE SCENARIO

Establishing clear and consistent procedures and transitions not only allows your classroom to run effectively, but is also crucial when something unexpected occurs.

In the following exercise, allow yourself to think in "worst-case scenarios," from minor setbacks to larger emergencies. Would you and your students know how to proceed during these scenarios? Should you have established transitions for unexpected situations? Consider the student behaviors you'd want to see in the examples below:

- There is an assembly in the auditorium in the middle of your Math Block.
- Your class heads outside for recess or an activity, and ten minutes in, it starts to thunderstorm.
- During a research activity in the library, the power goes out to that part of the school.
- There is an unexpected visitor on campus, and the school is put on lockdown.

ANCHOR ACTIVITIES

"What am I supposed to do now that I'm finished?" A successful teacher needs to anticipate this question from students and have activities planned for students who have completed their assigned work. In this video, Sharon reviews the importance of these anchor activities and explains how to use them to anchor students who might be drifting.

To watch this video, please visit:
https://youtu.be/9XYqRvk0wlw

CONCLUSION

As with any other classroom skill, students don't arrive already knowing how to navigate procedures and transitions. It's up to us as educators to teach them, just as you'd teach any other activity or task. First, determine how you want your class to run. Next, set expectations, demonstrate appropriate behaviors, and let students practice. Finally, continue to observe and support your students, and they'll be able to meet the high expectations for disciplined classroom behaviors as set forth by your procedures and transitions.

At this point, you've done most of the work necessary to set up your classroom for learning, including establishing the environment and how everything will work within that environment. Next, we'll discuss the specific actions you can take when students refuse to work within the environment you have created together.

PART THREE
RESPONDING TO MISBEHAVIOR

DISCIPLINED, FLEXIBLE, AND CALM

It's inevitable that issues with student behavior will arise. Some students have chronic histories of misbehavior, some have extenuating problems at home, and some simply love to test teachers and rules. Your approach to this misbehavior will be crucial to your success as a teacher.

The teacher with the most flexibility will have the most control where behavior is concerned. Your congruency and ability to respond to student misbehavior rather than escalate problems will improve both the efficacy of your teaching as well as your mental health.

Remember, discipline takes place in the classroom, not the administrator's office.

In this part, we will examine:

- **Responding to Chronic Misbehavior**

- **Dealing with Defiant Students**

- **Applying Case Studies for Specific Misbehaviors**

No teacher chooses their profession because they want to deal with misbehaving students, but it remains a critical aspect of your practice. When it comes to responding to misbehavior, we like this quote:

> "One looks back with appreciation to the brilliant teachers, but with gratitude to those who touched our human feelings. The curriculum is so much necessary raw material, but warmth is a vital element for the growing plant and for the soul of the child."
>
> CARL JUNG

INTRODUCTION TO RESPONDING TO MISBEHAVIOR

Dealing with misbehaving students is rarely any teacher's favorite part of the job, but arming yourself with the knowledge and strategies to defuse defiant students and regain control of your classroom is vital. In this video, Tony explains the importance of learning these skills and stresses that every student can be helped—it just takes a dedicated teacher.

To watch this video, please visit:
https://youtu.be/GbRHBtv_PFo

EIGHT

RESPONDING TO CHRONIC MISBEHAVIOR

Many student misbehaviors are either unintentional or too minor to require more than a reminder of the rule being broken. Many are correctable through a quick word of reprimand. Some students, however, chronically misbehave, violating classroom rules and procedures intentionally. These situations require a more considered approach.

The Response Pyramid for Chronic Misbehavior provides a model for responding to these students. While this model cannot guarantee success 100% of the time, it gives teachers the tools and strategies required to face regular and repeated misbehaviors.

Teachers should begin at the base of the Response Pyramid, employing Attention Moves.

If misbehavior continues, work your way up the Response Pyramid. If the misbehavior persists through continued interventions, it's advisable to notify the student's parents and draw up a behavior contract. You can find a sample behavior contract in this chapter.

RESPONSE PERIOD FOR CHRONIC MISBEHAVIOR

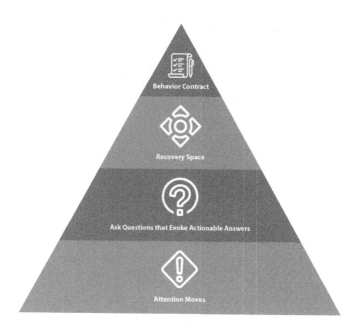

- **Attention Moves:** These are actions a teacher can take to capture or recapture the attention of their students. For most misbehavior, you will typically start here before escalating.
- **Ask Questions that Evoke Actionable Answers:** Don't ask students, "What are you doing?" Instead, ask students, "What should you be doing?" When the student responds, say, "Then do it now." Be sure to check on the student shortly afterward to ensure compliance.
- **Recovery Space:** If the unwanted behavior continues, the next step is to speak with the student and tell them if they don't get back to work, they'll have to

go to a time-out space and work alone. Important: keep students in the classroom where you can supervise them.

- **Behavior Contract:** If none of the actions suggested in the lower sections of the pyramid have worked, you can notify the parent and draw up a behavior contract. It's best if the student, parent, and counselor (if necessary) are involved in the creation of this document to increase the commitment to changing behaviors.

RESPONSE TECHNIQUES FOR MISBEHAVIOR

Different forms of classroom misbehavior require different responses. In this video, Tony brings you back into his simulated classroom to demonstrate the first two levels of the Response Pyramid for Chronic Misbehavior, and illustrates several ways to intervene with students misbehaving.

To watch this video, please visit:
https://youtu.be/_O66X7wfUrI

SAMPLE BEHAVIOR CONTRACT

Before executing a behavior contract, you should first check for and establish rapport with the student (if you don't already have it). With any behavior contract, you want to encourage the student's commitment to changing the undesired behavior. When seeking changes in behavior, go for small changes at first. Always allow students the opportunity to practice the desired behaviors they agreed to. This will increase the likelihood of a permanent change in behavior.

When employing the behavior contract, students need to understand that they're in an active partnership with you, the teacher. Through this partnership, the students recognize that they're responsible for their own behavior. Your role is more than that of a coach or consultant; you need to lead them through the questions on the contract and send the message that you believe in them and will support them through these changes. You'll assist them in drawing up the plan, while the student is in charge of actually implementing change.

Behavior Contract

1 - What rule did you violate?
_____

2 - What are three things you can do differently next time?
    1)_____
    2)_____
    3)_____

3 - Choose one of the behaviors and write what it would be like to do this new behavior. What will you:
    See - _____
    Hear - _____
    Feel - _____

4 - Are you going to do this? *Circle one:* Yes / No

5 - Do you need help from anyone to successfully behave in the new ways you have stated?
_____

6 - Imagine the next time you will be in a situation similar to the one that caused you to misbehave. When you turn in this behavior contract, we will discuss your plan to prevent it from happening again.

Please sign your name to this contract and I will send a copy to the school principal and your parent or guardian.

Student Name:_____

Guardian's Name:_____

Guardian's Approval:_____
                        (Sign Here)

Teacher's Name:_____

Class:_____

A

B

C

D

E

A) Make sure the student is specific and provides detailed information.

B) This will help your student build capacity for solution-oriented thinking.

C) Having the student visualize the alternate behavior helps the student embrace change.

D) Your student has already thought of solutions and visualized alternative behaviors. Now, you need to coach them through their plan and check for congruency.

E) Remember, the student is responsible for carrying out the agreement they created. A guardian's signature shows they agree with their child's plan for change.

MODEL CITIZENS

Most teachers accept that students need instruction, time, and practice to develop knowledge and skills. We gladly spend extra time in planning and lesson development to make sure that they "get it" when it comes to academics. Children aren't born knowing how to read, how to multiply, or how to behave. Why, then, do some teachers fall back on statements like "they should already know how to behave"?

The original goal for public education was the creation of an informed citizenry. All societies need good, law-abiding, responsible citizens, and as teachers, it's part of our responsibility to teach them these things! What are you doing to actively grow the necessary values and behaviors good citizens will need?

When you created your classroom rules, we asked that you tie them to values. Part of that process involved encouraging your students to identify values they admire in the people in their lives. Who are the positive role models your students admire? How can you compare or connect your students' misbehavior to their role model's good behavior?

NINE

DEALING WITH DEFIANT STUDENTS

More serious than the simple repeat offenders, defiant students are those who actively refuse to engage in the learning relationship between student and teacher. Regular consequences are often ineffective against defiant students, and so special techniques should be employed.

One Word Discipline

Defiant students rely on their defiance and misbehavior to throw educators off their teaching rhythms, either to disrupt the class or to achieve whatever it is they want. A powerful and effective strategy for resisting this is called the "One Word Discipline" approach.

The important feature of this approach is its congruency. No matter what the student says or does, the educator stays on message and does not change their approach.

The "One Word" you choose isn't important; what's important is that you remain unshakeable and unchanging in your conversation with the defiant student. The teacher refuses to be pulled into the student's arguments, putting up a verbal wall that the student is unable to overcome.

The reason this technique works is that it keeps you in control at all times. Most disciplinary interventions fail because the teacher gives up control in the student-teacher interaction, or because the teacher is indecisive, hesitant, or incongruous in their responses.

ONE WORD DISCIPLINE IN ACTION

How would you like to defuse defiant students with just one word? In this video, Tony demonstrates how to perform the One Word Discipline technique and explains how effective it can be in getting misbehaving students back on task. With this strategy in your teaching toolkit, you'll be able to maintain discipline in your classroom.

To watch this video, please visit:
https://youtu.be/iGjeNWweDFg

Student

I need to see my guidance counselor now so I can change my math class.

Why? This is important to me. I have to change my class.

That's not fair. Other teachers let students out of class.

I can't stand that word regardless!

Teacher

Regardless of what you have to do, sit in your seat and do your work.

Regardless of what is and what is not important, sit in your seat now.

Regardless of what's fair, I want you in your seat working now.

Nevertheless, sit in your seat now.

DEALING WITH MULTIPLE DEFIANT STUDENTS

This can be one of the most serious situations a teacher faces. With multiple students either defiant or willfully disrupting class, it can feel like your classroom is slipping out of your control. However, there are effective strategies for responding to groups of defiant students and regaining control of your class.

At the most basic level, if you're having repeated problems with defiant groups, you need to take inventory of what you've done thus far to create your classroom environment. Take time to reflect on and re-examine your rules and procedures to confirm that they are a good fit for your class and students. If so, take time during your school day to rehearse and review these rules with your class so they know them thoroughly.

Often, the problem of defiant groups can be distilled down to one highly defiant student influencing others. Speak to students one at a time after class, on separate days, to determine if there is indeed a group mindset devoted to disrupting you or if there's a ringleader encouraging others to make poor choices. If you can identify the student influencing the others, you can work to gain rapport and trust with them, and from there you can begin to foster more cooperation. If you can get the influencer on your side, they can positively use their influence to end the disruptions.

Above all, take defiant groups seriously. Good discipline happens in the classroom, but if things escalate to a dangerous or overwhelming level, you must seek help from an administrator. Remember to track student behavior diligently as these records will be a great help when dealing with administrators.

REMINDER CARDS

You can use colorful index cards with key messages to encourage appropriate student behavior. When a student is misbehaving, lay the corresponding card on their desk without comment or making it a big deal. If the misbehavior continues, simply walk by and point to the reminder card on their desk. Remove the card once the behavior has improved.

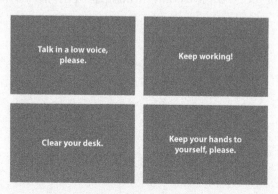

DIFFUSE DEFIANCE

Student misbehavior, as previously stated, may stem from a lack of control over a situation. The same can be applied to group misbehavior. When students are being influenced by one another, finding the root of the unwanted behavior can be a challenge, especially if the behavior is being fostered outside the classroom such as during lunch, on the bus, or during arrivals and dismissals from school.

Imagine your classroom has a group of students who continually get spoken to by lunchroom staff and monitors for their behavior in the cafeteria. Splitting these students up among different tables has shown little effectiveness.

What would your next steps be to identify the mentality of the group while working to dissipate the misbehaviors?

HOW STRONG IS YOUR NO?

Sooner or later, our more subtle and clever techniques for responding to misbehavior fail to produce results, and we simply have to tell them "no." How strong is your "no"? In this video, Tony leads an activity with a group of teachers, coaching them on how to develop a strong, resolved "no."

To watch this video, please visit:
https://youtu.be/GgKis4QAX7k

TEN
APPLYING CASE STUDIES FOR SPECIFIC MISBEHAVIORS

There are many possible responses to misbehaviors in your classroom. As a teacher, it's up to you to ensure your interventions are consistent, firm, and appropriate.

To provide a reference and a launching point for your thinking, presented on the next page are case studies for misbehaviors that highlight some of the most common misbehaviors you're likely to see in a classroom, along with some of the most effective responses.

THE STUDENT WHO IS CONSISTENTLY OFF TASK

- Walk over to the student and stand there quietly, using proximity as an attention move.
- Ask the student, "What are you supposed to be doing?"
- Hand the student a note that says, "Get to work."
- Talk privately with the student if this behavior persists and see if there is an explanation for the behavior.
- Whisper to the student, "Get on task."

THE STUDENT WHO CONSTANTLY DISRUPTS THE CLASS

- Review the classroom rules regarding respect or talking over someone.
- Remind the student of group discussion techniques.
- Conference with the student and discuss proper procedures and consequences if they are not followed.
- Have the student prepare a lesson to teach the rest of the class.

THE STUDENT WHO CAN'T GET ALONG WITH OTHER STUDENTS

- First, check for bullying or antagonizing from another student.
- Teach the student about social skills and working with others.
- Find another student who can work with the student and understands the issue at hand.
- Work on some bonding exercises with the entire group.
- Ask the school counselor for information on the student.

THE STUDENT WHO SEEKS ATTENTION USING NEGATIVE MEANS

- Record when the behavior takes place over time.
- Conference with the student to seek further information.
- Give the student tasks like running errands or collecting papers.
- Set up a signal with the student to use when the student is off task.
- Provide a study buddy.
- Remind the student of school rules that pertain to proper conduct.

THE PASSIVE STUDENT WHO WON'T PARTICIPATE

- Discuss privately with the student possible reasons for not participating and find out if the student needs help.
- Check with a counselor for personal or family problems.
- Find out if the student has a special skill that ties into the student's performance and build on that.
- Assign a study buddy to work with the student.
- Share organization strategies.

THE STUDENT WHO TALKS BACK

- Remain calm and slowly walk to the student. Look directly at the student and say softly, "That is not acceptable behavior."
- Walk away after that and stop about ten feet away. Look at the student and check for compliance.
- If the student gives you further problems, go back to the student and say you will deal with him/her after class. Continue teaching.
- Follow up with a brief conference right after class.

THE STUDENT WHO USES PROFANITY OR INAPPROPRIATE LANGUAGE

- Above all, remain calm. The way you respond is important for changing future behavior.
- Signal to the student to get on task. If the student complies, walk over and whisper in the student's ear to meet with you briefly after class.
- If the cursing continues, tell the student that cursing is prohibited and to get on task immediately or consequences will be enforced. If the student complies, walk over and whisper in the student's ear to meet with you briefly after class.
- If the cursing persists, send the student to the office and make sure the student gets there.
- Call the parent and report the infraction asking the parent to talk to the student.
- Have the student write a note to an adult they respect describing the incident.
- Have the student write a report on why people use profane language and the best way to control emotions.

THE STUDENT WHO WANTS CONTROL AND GETS UPSET AND ANGRY

- Remain calm and speak directly and emphatically.
- Difuse the anger first by saying, "I know you are upset now; what do you need to settle down?" If the request is reasonable, try to grant it.
- Send the student directly to the counselor if necessary.
- If the student gets too upset, isolate the student and keep saying, "You will be ok, just settle down." Lead the student away from the rest of the class to provide safe space.
- Give the student options to provide a way out. Say calmly with a stern voice, "Settle down. You can either sit in the back and not bother anyone or do an errand for me."
- Conference afterward and write a behavior contract for the student that discusses the anger problem.
- Provide the student with the opportunity to perform some relaxation exercises such as deep breathing, stretching, or journal writing.
- Recognize the student's positive behavior, too.

PICK A (MISBEHAVER) CARD,
ANY CARD

Consider the most common behaviors that come to mind when thinking about your classroom. Where do you find the most correction is needed?

Based on the case studies for misbehaviors on the previous pages, what are these students doing or wanting to achieve? Choose a couple of responses to implement over the course of two weeks. During this time, track and record how often you witness the behaviors you're trying to dispel. Revise your strategies as needed to fit your class.

CONSULT THE COUNSELOR

School counselors can be great partners to teachers. When you need help solving a problem centered on student needs, working with the school counselor can provide you with innovative solutions that address academic achievement.

When you notice warning signs, such as unusually poor grades or behavioral problems, school counselors can help you understand more about the student and the issues behind those behaviors. Also, if you ever feel like a situation concerning misbehavior is about to escalate, the school counselor can often prevent the problem from becoming too big.

Finally, school counselors can provide students with someone who will empathize with their personal problems and help them find solutions sensitive to their situation. If a student is having trouble getting along with you or other students, the school counselor can often broker peace and difuse the tension.

CONCLUSION

At the end of the day, classroom management is about getting students to do something (such as paying attention) or to stop doing something (such as being disruptive). Learning—not punishment—is the end goal. Defiant students need to be retaught how to perform in the classroom. The educator's goal is always for students to take responsibility for themselves by learning how to think critically and exercise self-control.

Sometimes we forget what it was like growing up. It's a difficult process, and one needs great support along the way. Talk to your students, build relationships with them, listen to what they say, and be curious about their behavior—both good and bad. It will pay off in the end.

At this point, you've created the environment and established the systems that will govern your classroom. Now, we can finally turn our attention to what you're going to teach!

LIFTOFF!

THE BEST CLASSROOM MANAGERS

Think of the great teachers that you know. Is it luck that they have the well-behaved, hardworking students, year in and year out? Of course not! What makes those teachers great is that they've learned *how* to create well-behaved, hardworking students, year in and year out. By learning some effective strategies to manage problematic behaviors in your classroom and committing yourself to their consistent application, you can begin to build a new environment for yourself and your students.

Your rules and consequences are the bedrock upon which you will construct your ideal classroom. Treat them almost like natural law and refer to them at every opportunity. Be specific in your wording and keep the language positive so that students know what actions they can take to show you that they want to meet your expectations. For the times when they are not meeting those expectations, have predictable, logical consequences that hold students accountable for their actions. Be sure to use consequences that won't damage the teacher-student relationship permanently.

Once you've established the parameters with your rules

and consequences, you'll need to train your students to operate within them. Procedures and transitions help keep order throughout the flow of activities in any given class. From handing in papers to bathroom visits, develop a clear vision for each common student action and how it should be performed in your classroom. Teach every learner the ideal performance and, when they become lax, reteach the ideal performance every single time! When your students know how your room works, the chaotic feel of those "in-between" moments will significantly lessen.

Finally, accept that there will be student misbehaviors. Be ready to respond with firm confidence showing that you are in control of your classroom. Remain flexible and meet each student misbehavior with an appropriate response. If you can remember that chronic misbehavior and defiance are more like clues than personal attacks against you, it will be easier to keep the proper perspective needed to manage unacceptable student behavior. Students will learn that you aren't going to meet their actions with impulsivity or anger but that you are no push-over. Be predictable and fair and you will show all students that you are trustworthy and safe.

Sometimes it can be hard to remember how much you love teaching—especially when most of your days consist of maintaining control of the classroom. If you feel this way, take heart—keep it simple and believe that improvement is possible! In the preceding chapters, you have learned all that you need to make a powerful change for yourself and your learners. Use it to lay the foundation for the kind of classroom you want and commit to any changes that you make. You can move beyond frustration and get back to doing what you love—teaching!

ABOUT THE AUTHORS

Dr. Anthony Scannella is the former CEO of the Foundation for Educational Administration, as well as an author, psychotherapist, and trainer in the field of neuropsychology. As the founder of The Principal Center for Educational Administration, Dr. Scannella has worked extensively with school administrators from the United States of America and abroad.

Sharon McCarthy is a national educational consultant and author. As president of Envision, Inc., Sharon works with stakeholders at all levels of the school system and has delivered professional development at the state, national, and international levels.

ALSO FROM EDUCATIONAL PARTNERS INTERNATIONAL

To view all of the videos included in this book, please visit our YouTube page:

https://www.YouTube.com/EducationalPartnersInternational

For additional professional development videos and resources, visit our website:

https://teachwithepi.com/professional-development

BIBLIOGRAPHY AND SUGGESTED READING

Blackerby, Don A. *Rediscover the Joy of Learning: With Blackerby's Academic Success Skills Tips*. Oklahoma City: Success Skills, 1996. Print.

Baumeister, Roy and John Tierney. *Willpower: Rediscovering the Greatest Human Strength*. New York: Penguin Group, 2012. Print.

Costa, Arthur and Bena Kallick, eds. *Activating & Engaging Habits of Mind*. Alexandria: ASCD, 2000. Print.

Costa, Arthur and Bena Kallick. *Assessment Strategies for Self-Directed Learning*. Thousand Oaks: Corwin, 2004. Print.

Dennison, Paul E. and Gail E. Dennison. *Brain Gym: Simple Activities for Whole Brain Learning*. Ventura: Edu-Kinesthetics, 1992. Print.

Dilts, Robert B. and Todd L. Epstein. *Dynamic Learning*. Capitola: Meta Publications, 1995. Print.

Duhigg, Charles. "Group Study." *New York Times Magazine* 28 Feb. 2016: 20-30. Print.

Dweck, Carol. *Mindset*. New York: Ballantine, 2016. Print.

Garner, Betty. *Getting to Got It!: Helping Struggling Students How to Learn*. Alexandria: ASCD, 2007. Print.

Guber, Tara. and Leah Kalish. *Yoga Pretzels: 50 Fun Yoga Activities for Kids and Grownups.* Bath: Barefoot, 2005. Print.

Hattie, John and Helen Timperley. "The Power of Feedback." *Review of Educational Research* 77.1 (2007): 81-112. Print.

Jahren, Hope. *Lab Girl.* New York: Alfred A. Knopf, 2016. Print.

Marzano, Robert J. *The Art and Science of Teaching: A Comprehensive Framework for Effective Instruction.* Alexandria: ASCD, 2007. Print.

Meyer, Anne, David H. Rose, and David Gordon. *Universal Design for Learning: Theory and Practice.* Wakefield: CAST, 2014. Print.

Middendorf, Joan and Alan Kalish. "The Change Up in Lectures." *The National Teaching and Learning Forum* 5.2 (1996): 1-5. Print.

Newberg, Andrew and Mark Robert Waldman. *Words Can Change You Brain: 12 Conversation Strategies to Build Trust, Resolve Conflict, and Increase Intimacy.* New York: Penguin, 2013. Print.

O'Hanlon, Bill. *Do One Thing Different: Ten Simple Ways to Change Your Life.* New York: Harper Collins, 2019. Print.

Payne, Ruby. *Research-Based Strategies: Narrowing the Achievement Gap for Under-Resourced Students.* Highlands: aha! Process, 2017. Print.

Prensky, Marc. *Teaching Digital Natives: Partnering for Real Learning.* Thousand Oaks: Corwin, 2010. Print.

Pryor, Karen. *Don't Shoot the Dog: The New Art of Teaching and Training.* Lydney: Ringpress, 2002. Print.

Scannella, Anthony. *Changing Student Behavior: Comprehensive Learning and Interventions for Correcting Kids.* Lanham: Rowman & Littlefield, 2007. Print.

Scannella, Anthony and Sharon McCarthy. *Innovative Interventions for Today's Exceptional Children: Cultivating a Passion for Compassion.* Lanham: Rowman & Littlefield, 2009. Print.

Sharron, Howard and Martha Coulter. *Changing Children's Minds: Feuerstein's Revolution in the Teaching of Intelligence.* Highlands: aha! Process, 2004. Print.

Vygotsky, L.S. *Mind in Society: The Development of Higher Psychological Processes.* Cambridge: Harvard UP, 1978. Print.

Willis, Judy. *Research-Based Strategies to Ignite Student Learning: Insights from a Neurologist and Classroom Teacher.* Alexandria: ASCD, 2006. Print.

NOTES

Made in the USA
Coppell, TX
28 July 2022

80569629R00063